Mikey Discovers His
SUPER POWER

LORENA DOLINAR, RP
ILLUSTRATIONS BY OLGA BARINOVA

◆ FriesenPress

Suite 300 - 990 Fort St
Victoria, BC, V8V 3K2
Canada

www.friesenpress.com

Copyright © 2019 by Lorena Dolinar, RP
First Edition — 2019

All rights reserved.

No part of this publication may be reproduced in any form, or by any means, electronic or mechanical, including photocopying, recording, or any information browsing, storage, or retrieval system, without permission in writing from FriesenPress.

"To improve lives, build community and ignite action."
A portion of the proceeds of this book will be donated to United Way Halton & Hamilton.

The opinions and content of this book are independent from those of United Way Halton & Hamilton.

The information offered in this book should not be used as source to replace any consultation, assessment, or treatment by a qualified health professional.

ISBN
978-1-5255-3611-3 (Hardcover)
978-1-5255-3612-0 (Paperback)
978-1-5255-3613-7 (eBook)

1. Juvenile Nonfiction, Health & Daily Living, Daily Activities

Distributed to the trade by The Ingram Book Company

Dedication

This book is dedicated to all children, to inspire them to discover their natural superpower, which will allow them to embrace the present moment and live life mindfully. I give special thanks to my husband, Rob, and our two children, Damir and Danijela, who first inspired me to write this book. It was their continued love and support that made it possible to write and share this story.

Mikey and his friend Nia are besties. They are in Ms. DeVitto's Grade 4 class together. They are neighbours and have been good friends for a long time.

However, they do not always

See the World in the same way.

Nia loves to enjoy life in the moment. She calls this "being mindful," and it is her superpower!

Nia practices mindfulness in many ways . . .

She likes taking the time to smell the flowers in the garden.

She likes dancing in her living room.

She especially loves to show kindness to others.

Nia feels powerful, because she can quiet her mind when her thoughts go in a direction she does not want them to go. Instead of worrying about what will happen at school tomorrow, she will settle her mind by using meditation. It is a mindfulness practice that allows her to bring her thoughts into the present moment.

Her friend Mikey often misses out on his chance to enjoy life in the moment. Unlike Nia, he is unable to let go of his fears. He just worries, and worries, and keeps worrying.

Most days, Mikey is afraid to leave his house to play outside.

He feels nervous when he is around other kids, because sometimes they say mean things and then laugh at him.

He would like to have more friends but he finds it hard to talk to other kids.

He is always worried that something bad will happen, like falling off his bicycle and getting hurt.

Mikey is so afraid that he spends hours playing games on his tablet. He has no clue that the day is passing him by. Sometimes his mother has to call his name for dinner five times before he finally hears her.

Nia notices that Mikey does not seem very happy. She wonders if she can help him learn to enjoy his life more and worry less.

She begins to think, and think, and really think . . .

And then a thought comes to her. She realizes she can teach him about his superpower, the superpower that everyone has: mindfulness!

Nia knows that Mikey can handle his worries better just by being mindful; all it takes is some practice. She also knows that anyone can use this superpower if they are willing to practice. She believes he can overcome his fears with the power of being mindful!

Nia heads out to find Mikey and tell him her exciting news. Her superpower turns on! She notices she is, in this moment, skipping along the sidewalk to Mikey's house.

She has a big smile on her face.

Nia finds Mikey at his home. He is crying in his bedroom. She feels concerned and asks, "What is the matter, Mikey?"

Mikey explains that his mom got upset with him because he spends too much time on his tablet, so she took it away for awhile. Now he feels badly about what happened, but also very bored, too. "Nia," he sobs, "I am a lousy kid. I just don't know what to do." Nia says she knows how bad it can feel when parents get upset, and gives him a big warm hug.

In the next moment, she gives Mikey a gentle look and calmly says, "Don't worry, my friend, I know how to help you." She feels a burst of excitement as she tells him that he has a superpower! She says, "Mikey, you just need to learn how to use it."

Mikey feels unsure. He asks Nia, "What superpower do I have?"

She tells him it is a superpower everyone has, called

MINDFULNESS.

Mikey takes a long pause. As usual, he begins to worry, and worry, and worry. His thoughts tell him, *I can't do it*, and *I am not good at anything*.

"Mindfulness can only work if you're willing to learn it," Nia says. "Do you want to give it a try?"

"Okay," Mikey carefully agrees. "I'll give it a try."

To encourage Mikey, Nia says, "I believe in you. I know you have this superpower inside of you . . . I just know it."

Mikey's eyes widen with happiness. He feels comforted that his friend is by his side. He is not aware that in this moment his mood is already beginning to change.

He asks Nia,

"HOW CAN I LEARN HOW TO USE MY SUPERPOWER?"

"It can be tricky at first," she explains, "but allow me to take you to a wonderful place called 'the present moment.'" She says, "Come sit with me and I will tell you what I mean."

"Close your eyes and listen to my voice.
Take a breath in. Take a breath out.
Become aware of your breath.
Slowly breathe in and out.
What do you see right now?
What thoughts come into your mind?
When you have a thought, let the thought pass through you,
Just like how the wind comes and passes by.
Think about how the wind doesn't stay forever.
Sometimes there are strong wind gusts, and sometimes there are light breezes.
But remember how the wind always passes by.
Let your thoughts be like the wind.
They will come, and they will go.
Always look and take notice of them,
but don't hang on to them for long.

Keep your Mind open
to the next thought that will come."

Mikey and Nia sit in silence for a few moments.

Then suddenly something begins to happen. Thoughts come into Mikey's mind. He is watching them as they come one by one.

Now, Mikey notices that he is no longer crying.

Now, Mikey realizes that Nia is sitting in his room with him.

And now, Mikey notices that he is starting to feel better.

"Did you notice your superpower in action?" Nia asks.

"I do, I do see my superpower!" Mikey replies cheerfully. "I can see how one thought goes to another thought. Instead of holding on to a thought, I can choose to let the thoughts pass by.

So when I am mindful I can be in control of what I THINK about!"

This is an amazing day. Mikey has discovered that his own mind is his superpower! He realizes that by being aware of what is happening in the present moment, he can open his mind to see the world differently. He has learned that being mindful can make any problem a little easier to handle. Thinking mindfully, Mikey imagines what tools he will use to help him make up with his mom.

He doesn't feel stuck in his sadness anymore!

Nia is thrilled for Mikey! She tells him that being mindful is something he can do at any moment, anytime, and anywhere. She says, "This power gets stronger the more you make an effort to use it. Mindfulness is like an exercise for your brain, just like running is exercise for your heart." Then Nia tells him the best part. "Mindfulness can help you in so many ways, like making choices and handling your feelings. It's much easier to remember things when you practice mindfulness, and you will be able to focus your mind better."

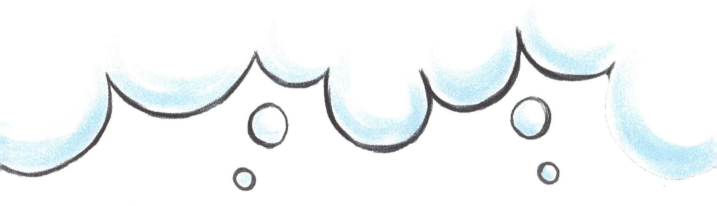

Then she takes a breath and says,
"Oh, and I almost forgot. Mindfulness will keep you in

With Nia's guidance, Mikey is super-excited to learn more about mindfulness. He knows it won't be easy, and that it will take lots of practice. He wants to get better at it, so he makes the effort to use his new-found superpower everywhere and every day.

Mikey is able to sort out his argument with his mom using mindfulness. He decides he will take the first step, telling her he is sorry. Then he tells her he will try harder to be on his tablet less. She is really pleased with his ability to resolve the problem in such a helpful way. He notices, after they talk it through, that he and his mom

start getting along MUCH better!

He also begins to use mindfulness during car rides with his parents. He happily looks out the car window to observe the other cars, the buildings, the trees, and the clouds in the sky.

Mikey loves to see shapes in the clouds!

He loves to practice his superpower at bedtime. Lying in his bed before he falls asleep, he focuses his mind on his breathing. When he notices that he is beginning to think about something else, he brings his mind back to focus on his breathing again, and again, and again. Mikey calls this mindfulness practice

"the breathing game."

He practices his superpower at school, too. He works hard to be present in the moment, to focus on what the teacher is saying. Just as Nia explained, he listens to Ms. DeVitto's voice very closely. He tries to follow every word she is saying. Sometimes Mikey acts silly and doesn't pay attention, and then he gets sent down to the office. He knows he has to work extra hard to stay in control of his mind so that he can

Stay out of trouble.

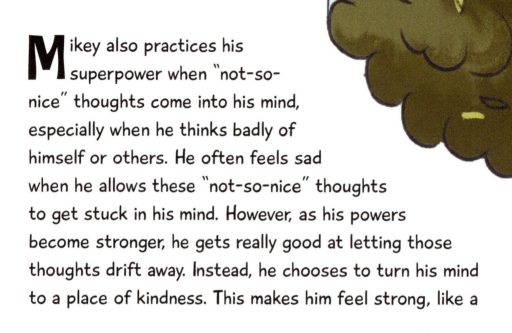

Mikey also practices his superpower when "not-so-nice" thoughts come into his mind, especially when he thinks badly of himself or others. He often feels sad when he allows these "not-so-nice" thoughts to get stuck in his mind. However, as his powers become stronger, he gets really good at letting those thoughts drift away. Instead, he chooses to turn his mind to a place of kindness. This makes him feel strong, like a

Superhero!

Mikey's superpower makes him feel like he has just finished climbing the highest mountain on Earth.

He is more willing to try new adventures, and his fears no longer stand in his way.

He spends less time on his tablet and finds other ways to enjoy his day.

He especially likes to be helpful to others. This makes him feel all warm and fuzzy inside.

And best of all, he can quiet the worries in his mind.

Mikey feels grateful to Nia for showing him all the different ways he can use mindfulness in his life. He loves his superpower because it frees his mind from fear, sadness, and pain. He sees the world in a whole new way because he has the power to be in control of his thoughts, feelings, and actions in every moment. He has discovered that being mindful is the beginning to living a healthy life and finding happiness along the way.

Mikey strongly believes that there is no greater superpower than the mighty

POWER OF MINDFULNESS!

A Note to Parents and Teachers

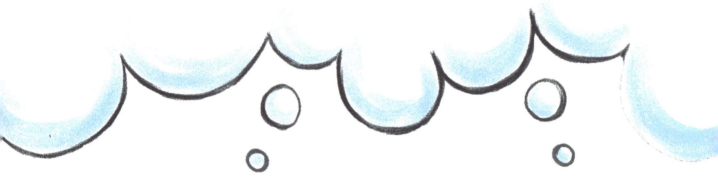

The purpose of this book is to introduce children to the concept of mindfulness and the important role it has in daily life. This story can be used as a guide for discussion with children and to build their understanding about what being mindful looks like. My hope is that children can relate to the characters, recognize the value of mindfulness in improving their overall happiness and wellness, and make mindfulness a regular daily practice.

Here are some questions to consider asking your child after reading the story:

1. What was your favourite part of the story?

2. Do you feel more like Mikey or Nia? Why?

3. What did you learn from the story?

4. How do you think mindfulness could help you if you practiced?

5. Can you think of a time when you were being mindful?

6. How did using mindfulness help you feel better or look at a situation differently?

In today's society, there is an increasing concern about mental health and well-being. There are many distractions, and we are all impacted by the level of access we have to so much information. With the evolution of technology (such as smartphones and social media) and the greater role it has in daily life, there seems to be a growing inability to cope with stress, especially in the children and adolescents who are growing up within this culture. Teaching mindfulness to young children has become more necessary in our rapidly changing society.

I was inspired to write this fun and relatable story as a practical resource for parents and teachers to guide them in helping children develop their mindfulness skills. My ultimate goal and hope for this book is that children will begin to develop vocabulary, knowledge, and understanding about concepts related to mental health, empathy, mindfulness, wellness, and self-compassion. In addition, parents and teachers who can model these skills will help foster a child's development of self-awareness while also empowering them to understand how they can cope effectively in life.

Mindfulness is a way of living intentionally with awareness of the present moment while letting go of judgments. To develop this skill, choose a mindfulness practice. One that is commonly used is focusing on your breath. After practicing it yourself, introduce the mindfulness practice to the child. Explain all the instructions to the child before you begin. Invite the child to sit in a comfortable position (they may or may not choose to close their eyes), and then instruct them to breathe in and out, focusing only on their breath. Tell them they will notice that they will become distracted and their attention/thoughts will move away from their breath. Reassure the child it is normal for the mind to wander. Ask them to simply notice this, but then bring their attention back to breathing in and out. Instruct them to keep doing this over and over again for the duration of the practice (one to three minutes, depending on the age or ability of the child). They may also notice some concerns over whether or not they are doing it correctly, but tell them it's important to simply notice that they have drifted from focusing on their breathing. Ask them to try to let go of that thought and to shift their attention back to their breath each time. Also keep in mind that for the duration of the practice, you and your child are silent. It may help to use a mindfulness bell to start and end the practice. In the story, Mikey refers to this practice as "the breathing game." Framing it this way may help engage the child in a way that can be fun.

After the mindfulness practice is over, you can discuss with your child what the experience was like for them. You can simplify the language, but here are some questions you can consider for discussion with your child:

1. Did you notice willingness or unwillingness to participate in the practice?

2. What did you notice while you were focusing on your breathing?

3. Did you notice that your thoughts went somewhere else, or that you were not able to sit still, which distracted you from your breathing?

4. Despite being distracted at any point during the practice, were you able to bring your attention back to your breathing?

It's important to share with the child your own experience of doing the mindfulness practice, as well. Offer reassurance that mindfulness practice can be challenging, and let them know it can get easier with practice. Additionally, it is important to try different types of mindfulness practices (e.g., drawing a picture or colouring a picture: see the list of examples provided), because some practices may work better than others. Following the instructions above, you can try different activities on which to focus the mind. When the feeling of unwillingness arises, explore with your child how to shift from being unwilling to willing to try an exercise. Often judgements underlie unwillingness to participate. Gently encourage your child to notice these judgments when they arise and then help them work toward letting go of judgemental thoughts. In other words, letting go of judgemental thoughts is an important part of being able to fully engage in an experience and to be present in the moment.

You can also suggest other practices they would be more willing and open to try. Remember that these concepts will take time to develop because children are still in the early stages of developing their self-awareness. Using the language and labelling for your child when you observe them to be mindful may be a great place to begin in supporting the development of mindfulness skills.

Developing these skills and abilities in children is an ongoing learning process. Seeking out additional resources online, other books, or help from a qualified health professional can further enrich the progress of a child's development of mindfulness skills, along with other positive coping skills.

Examples of mindfulness practice:

Colouring a picture	Singing
Drawing a picture (e.g. flower, or dog)	Word search puzzle
Dancing	Jigsaw puzzle
Stargazing	Eating a piece of candy/chocolate
Write a list of "most favourite things"	Alphabet games

About the Author

Lorena Dolinar is an author, mother, and registered psychotherapist. She holds an honours degree from the University of Toronto in psychology, as well as an addictions diploma from Georgian College. She has worked as a substance use therapist for over seventeen years. She has also been trained in mindfulness, and she teaches this skill to youth accessing counselling services. Her work reflects her deep concern for kids growing up in today's fast-paced and uncertain world, as well as her dedication to helping others. She believes that mindfulness is an effective starting point for regaining a sense of calm and control and improving daily functioning. "Mikey Discovers His Superpower" is her first book. She currently lives in Oakville, Ontario, with her husband and two children, as well as the family's miniature pinscher, Bella.

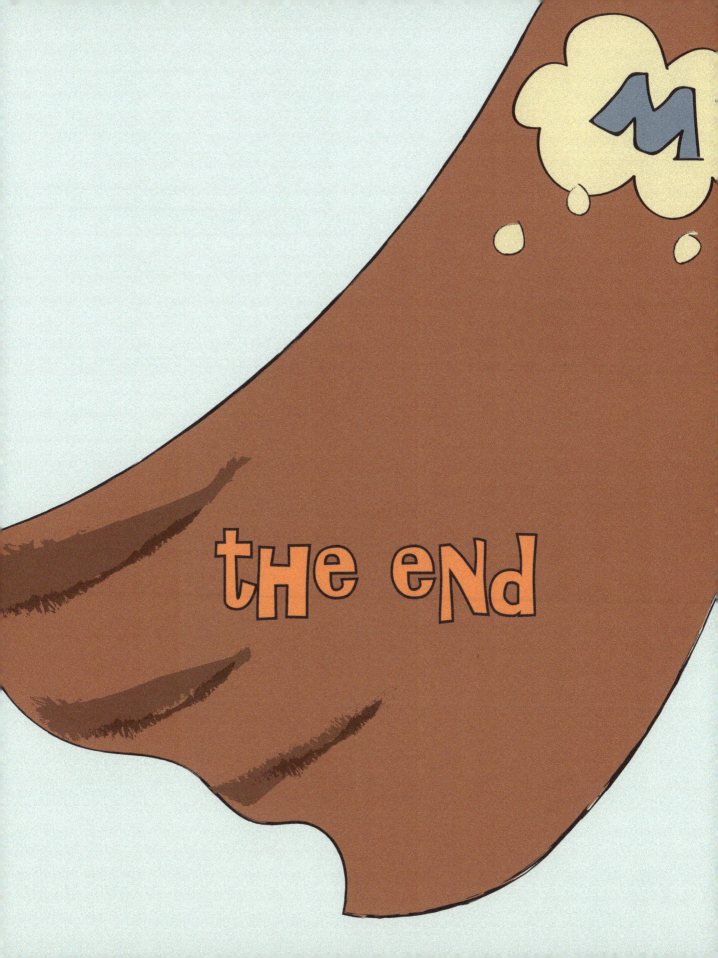

CPSIA information can be obtained
at www.ICGtesting.com
Printed in the USA
LVHW051034290519
619350LV00002B/2/P